NOTES ON

ARRIVAL

AND DEPARTURE

BOOKS BY RACHEL ROSE

Giving My Body to Science (1999)
Notes on Arrival and Departure (2005)

NOTES ON

ARRIVAL

AND DEPARTURE

RACHEL ROSE

Copyright © 2005 by Rachel Rose

Library and Archives Canada Cataloguing in Publication

Rose, Rachel, 1970-
Notes on arrival and departure / Rachel Rose.

Poems.
ISBN 0-7710-7591-X

I. Title.

PS8585.07325N68 2005   C811'.54   C2004-906723-0

We acknowledge the financial support of the Government of Canada through the Book Publishing Industry Development Program and that of the Government of Ontario through the Ontario Media Development Corporation's Ontario Book Initiative. We further acknowledge the support of the Canada Council for the Arts and the Ontario Arts Council for our publishing program.

The epigraph to "Notes on Arrival and Departure" on page 30 is from "Oh Earth, Wait for Me," from *Selected Poems: A Bilingual Edition* by Pablo Neruda, edited by Nathaniel Tarn, translated by Anthony Kerrigan, W.S. Merwin, Alistair Reid, and Nathaniel Tarn. Copyright © 1970, 1975. Published by Penguin Books.

The epigraph to "Stars" on page 45 is from "Detached Verses," from *Sloan-Kettering: Poems* by Abba Kovner, translated by Eddie Levenston. Copyright © 2002 by the Estate of Abba Kovner. Used by permission of Schocken Books, a division of Random House, Inc.

Text design by Sean Tai
Typeset in Minion by M&S, Toronto
Printed and bound in Canada

This book is printed on acid-free paper that is
100% ancient-forest friendly (100% post-consumer recycled).

McClelland & Stewart Ltd.
The Canadian Publishers
481 University Avenue
Toronto, Ontario
M5G 2E9
www.mcclelland.com

1 2 3 4 5   09 08 07 06 05

for Isabelle, for Benjamin and Gabrièle
mes brins d'amour

CONTENTS

NOTES ON
ARRIVAL
AND DEPARTURE

AMERICAN PAGEANT

How we applauded you, pint-sized tart
singing and swinging to "A Cowboy's Sweetheart."
Who taught you the art of sashay, of rouge,
the French manicure? Who taught you to bruise?
Who bleached your pearly teeth before each show?
Who curled your tinted hair and tied the bow?

We can offer you nothing, especially not the promise
it won't happen again. JonBenet, angel, one request:
If you see the Smith boys floating around those parts
tell them that Susan still dots her "i's" with little hearts
in all her prison letters. Tell them she confessed.
A mother who put her shoulder to her work, paused to rest,

pushed. The boys were asleep in the back until they woke
to a lake pierced by headlights, birth in reverse.
There was no phantom African, no dark abductor,
though we pictured him standing where she stood onshore.
Water poured through windows, flooded the cocoon.
Silence of a woman alone with the moon.

WOMAN BEING TRANSFUSED BY A GOAT

Musée de la Médecine, Paris, 1807

The goat's already dead, its neck-blood drained
into your quiet arm hung from the table edge.
Blood stains your gown, glass tubes are pressed to your veins
in this last mad experiment of hemorrhage
reversal. Some unknown artist painted you
an unrepentant flirt, dishevelled bodice open
to let your marbled breasts shine through,
all your black hair unbound, undone,
caressing the transfuser's overcoat
as he puzzles in top hat and gloves. You're pale foil
to a black goat with devilish hooves, slit throat,
bloodied lolling tongue. Your lips are parted as though
you wished to speak of this wilder salty blood.
You would have refused transfusion. You would have been ignored.

TABLE OF EARS

Musée de la Médecine, Paris

An ebony table inlaid with ears
whispers of the bargains made to make it.
An ear for its weight in bread, in gold;
poorhouse corpses disinterred and sold.
The table is dark and very old, one upon which
the Marquis de Sade would have been proud
to rest his hat, his calling card. It is a table of reductions,
the piece the maid always dusted last, though the canals
were hard to clean. *Hush*: between the lacquered ear inlays,
in luminous suspension, green rococo of mantis prays,
plays tricks on the eye. Set between the severed ears
and flowers composed entirely of knuckles,
between the ivory knots of human vertebrae,
jewel beetles' metallic bodies gleam in vertiginous display.

GIFT OF TONGUES

How dangerous your life is
between the walls of wet teeth
and the chasm we call throat.
Life is sweet at the beginning,
bitter and sour in the middle, and finally tasteless
at the end of it all. O the way you curl when I ask you
to say *mulberry*, say *cunnilingus*,
the way you tremble and wet yourself
at the sour anticipation of lemon tarts.

You have fed me well, satisfied my lovers, told my stories.
Your hinge has been wounded against sharp pearls,
the price for stretching full length
in pleasure. You have caught the bitter
draught of men, the rolling pungency of women,
and after, in the quiet room,
you have lifted yourself from where you lay,
pressed your tip against the palate's chapel
and formed the word *Love*.

Tonight, eating curled squid cross-hatched with diamonds,
I bit right through you. I believed you tougher than that.
My throat filled as you swelled and swelled.
Panting, my mouth open and spilling blood,
I gave birth to hunger, abstinence, silence.

It was only when mute that you revealed
the wound that can't be stitched must be concealed.

EEL

The war continues. We just want you dead, the end
of your species, genocide. Scourge of the Everglades,
you are too full of bones, you are self-sufficiency incarnate,
stubborn hermaphrodite, upsetting the natural order.
We set the terms through which you slip,
trick-knot, freestyle, make your escape
from someone's tank or bucket, intent
on the only true revenge: annihilation.

Still, perversely, we admire what we can't kill.
First your sex: spiny shape-shifter,
born male but becoming female,
impregnating yourself whenever it
suits you. When we add poison to your waters
you merely lift your sleek chiselled head
and breathe air, you seek out the delicate eggshells
of ibis and egret, catch mice, hunt fish.

When we drain the swamps, your nature changes,
you leave fish-self behind and become snake.
Land-dweller, you slither for miles on your belly through the dark,
hooded eyes gleaming. Bolder than Thoreau, you need nothing.

You have no pretensions and we have not learned
what you might teach us: sewer pipe or pristine lake,
wherever your world, you claim. You swallow
your tail and roll like a wheel to escape fire,
rear your young in the bloated bodies
of drowned livestock. Each spring brings swarms
of intestinal blissful reunion, over
and under the rib cages, the gas-burst flesh,
revelling in the fecund darkness, knowing
you, above all creatures, have been blessed.

Dark Flags

When my bay mare was in heat, we no longer
loved each other. She pranced her desperation,
rolling the broken bit between her teeth, wanting,
not wanting, grieved. Her black tail snapped

jazz, saucy whip beating time against her flanks
as the rosy mollusc of her vulva began its show.
The winking. Clenching, declenching –
even the geldings feigned interest.

I rode her with blunt spurs,
my old mare of ten foals, but steel's bite
meant nothing when we passed the stallion run.
All along the fence, her own

young stallions raced, pricked
ears at her scent, bugled their calls.
She flared the red mucosa of her nostrils,
tossed her head, flashed and flashed the mollusc.

The whole ungelded herd shifted, swerved,
gauging the cracking fence,
and then her one sienna son
lifted his sinewed neck and flew:

     A magician's
    cape   red and black
   a silk   tarp
quick   as voltage.

Other stallions flung up turf, hoisted the long bones
of their tails, brushed dark flags along electric
fence, screamed. The sienna one silently crossed,
teeth bared, closed the space between us.

I knew nothing of desire then, except fear,
and I leaned down and beat my heels against it.
My mare lashed out with polished hooves, knocked blood
onto her son's startled face, opened a path for us.

We got to the barn. The men came running, the mad vaulter
was caught, corralled. Jack and Martin spit tobacco juice
into the dust, called the jumper *you sonuvabitch*,
split an apple with their pocket knives,

and held the pieces to his whiskered lips.
My mare and I trembled as I walked the heat out,
scraped lather from her steaming neck.
Still her vulva winked its fleshy black and pink

unbroken dance, coy, demanding to be covered,
and I tossed a cooling blanket over her bruised sides,
walked her in slow circles,
the heat still rising.

Not until she dropped her head and nuzzled me there
did I feel the sting of my own blood,
pucelle no more, and divined what I'd lost
against a Western saddle's gleaming pommel.

October Stroller

We have never tried so hard for anything. We've tried
for years. Now I walk alone around the lake.
My longing congeals into monthly clots of blood,
sheds itself. Sugar maples shed their scarlet in dark water.
The last invitation was offered
only two days before. *It's too early to tell,*

I say to myself, *too early to tell.*
There are few options we haven't tried.
With each failure, the doctors offer
less hope. Grief is twilight at a man-made lake.
Children throw bread on the water
for the jewelled mallards. I lick my chapped lips, blood

seeps from the cracks. I don't care about blood
bonds, I just want a child to whom I can tell
my grandmother's stories. Water
reflects my face in broken waves. All year I've tried
singing one forth; now I am mute. A stroller in the lake
glints, and an old woman points it out, offers

her theory to passersby. *Pity,* she murmurs, and I offer
no reply. The stroller sparkles, while blood-
coloured leaves rock beneath the surface of the lake.
The story of barrenness is an endless retelling;
I have told it too many times. It is hard to keep trying
and I live at a distance, I live as though moving through water.

It's October; this darkening body of water
swallows and drowns each appeal I offer.
I never imagined myself in an ordered house. I try
so hard to stop my own blood's
coming. A single turtle floats, blinks, tells
me nothing. Sleep will come soon under a frozen lake,

the wait for a warmer season. Its heart will slow; the lake
will ice its lids shut. The stroller will sink a little deeper underwater.
I've tried to slow down my heart. I've considered telling
my story to an old woman. Has that stroller been offered
as a final clue, a message encrypted like blood
on morning sheets? My desire beckons, inchoate, tries

to tell the same story with a new ending. Lake,
let me in. I have been tried and sentenced to water
and solitude. Must blood be offered for blood?

The Proof

The second heart in my body
beats lower down, twice as fast
as the first one. It will be yours
when you split off from me
to become yourself;
at least this is the theory.
You are still a beloved conjecture,
an equation awaiting proof.

The first sign is how you sicken me,
bile rising in my throat
as I crunch the roasted wings
of ducks and chickens.
How many birds consumed
to create your placenta alone? The equation
is bone upon bone of sacrifice
and the outcome
far from certain. The proof is this:

I grow heavy with your expanding
vesselature, plush and pulsing
as an eye socket, and you the eye.
Already your hands beat against me,
measuring confinement.
And who can solve the riddle of what spark
jump-started your heart,
provided the first electric impulse?

You are inexplicable
as the creation of the world,
the primeval clot that begins to beat,
grow limbs and leave the water, develop
opposable thumbs. Soon your blood
will circulate its course against my own,
pulsing double time in the blue flax
of your fine veins. Soon
you will not be contained.

The life I had before
will be as unbelievable to you
as silent movies.
The faith is this: that the division
of me into you
will be an odd one,
the algebra imperfect, that
there will be a remainder.

Triple Crown

Cage a monarch in your two
hands, wings beating amber
pollen, light as breath against your fingertips,
hot wishes ticking in your hips.

Catch a green toad, throbbing
in its fear and prodigious strength,
and when you are ready
release your deep-throated desire
to the amnios, to the amphibian chorus.

Canter bravely to the salt edge
though you've never ridden a running horse
before, the ache between your legs
from the pounding, brine air, tang of whipped
hair against your chapped lips, lather
on his dark neck thick as the foam
flinging itself up the wet shoreline, God love you,
it is time, he has taken the reins –

Cling to him with no way of stopping
sand tossed beneath sharp hooves, you just have to breathe
and hold on, you just have to hold on and breathe
until you reach the cliffs and together have run
the whole incredible distance, you have made
good time. Who wouldn't tremble?
Go ahead: tremble as you dismount,
begin to walk the heat out, still

joined by the leather cord of the bridle,
foam drying to a vernix of milksalt,
the Apgar of the run a perfect ten.

Two Roads Diverged

And sorry I could not travel both
And be one traveler . . .
    – Robert Frost, "The Road Not Taken"

for Masarah

As a girl you were dangerous, sharp-edged, alone
and so much like me in your need for the outlawed and the wild.
Now I have become good; every night I sleep at home.
And you still run wild, though you've grown
wise to men if not to yourself. At thirty, we find ourselves both "with child,"

to put it delicately, though mine is a plan fantastically created,
yours, a mistake. I slept hard this afternoon, baby shifting inside,
fists skittering like mice in the ribs of a barn. I've waited
long years for this, though my fears have not abated:
ambivalence wraps me in a drowning tide,

and I wake thinking of you, sleeping off the cramp, your
friends and lovers barred entry. How carefully you spoke
of it the day I stopped by, unsure
how to help you bear this as each day brings me closer to labour,
and you unsure what you could say. Finally your voice broke.

You sat on the old green couch and began to rock,
predicted a life of poverty and despair.
Your reluctance to talk
of loss in the face of my long infertility. Your door locked.
But souls have passed through us. Did you fear

yourself a dark spell, evil eye? Taking the path that leads the other way,
I am also walking with you. If you can't face this quickening swell
I understand. I'm with you anyway.
I'll leave my foolish bouquet
to wilt on your balcony. I'll leave as well

the promise not to speak of this for a time,
until you are ready to catch my son, hold him. A woman
is defined by what she will and will not bear. I trust in time
you'll be okay. Comfort yourself with poems, verse in rhyme
where the order matters, where no word is accidental. Come undone

for a while, if you must; unburden yourself with free verse.
Two roads diverged, and you? And I?
We walk our separate paths, bent in the undergrowth. Ghosts
of the future and ghosts of the past
cling to our hips in the tall wet grass.

SICKBED

Pregnant and in bed with influenza,
a different strain than killed Grandfather's fiancée
while he fought in World War I, feet rotting in the trenches.
He enlisted at sixteen, lied his way

to Europe to learn to be a man. Within the year
he was shot down. While he recovered, her letters stopped.
He heard from her sister how the fever consumed her,
then, after a week, dropped her – cavalier courtier! –

waxberry white against her pillows. He limped home
to hang up his uniform, married her sister instead.
Of course he wasn't the same. On winter nights he'd moan,
caught in dreams of being shot. She'd wake and wait for dawn.

Was it ghosts of his dead love that haunted him?
Buried while carrying his child, illegitimate unborn
secret. (Was that one meant to be my father?)
The leftover sister, barren, tired of seeking love

where there was no love, deserted.
He stayed in New York, cultivated drink, flirted
with suicide, finally married the woman
who became my grandmother, light-slippered

Jewish orphan fresh off the boat. She was a lucky one,
scant years between her escape and another Great War.
I've heard how they could drink, how alcohol
was their favoured child, how her eyes grew black and wild,

she who turned her back on God,
whose family sat shiva for her when she married
outside the tribe. He never got over the war,
a coward, according to my father, afraid of the dark,

of losing his children if they left the house.
They survived, took their places in the world,
this world which lumbers on despite us.
God, I'm tired, the sun's setting on this blasted winter day,

fever washes my bones. I settle back into the pillows, lumpen,
secure – influenza doesn't kill us any more.
Though perhaps it will. To whom must I pray?
The baby knocks my ribs, hammers my civilian complacency –

due to be born on the cusp of yet another war.

Passing Through Evolution

Urge, and urge, and urge,
Always the procreant urge of the world.
    – Walt Whitman, "Leaves of Grass"

If I could, on your coming-of-age trip,
I'd sit by your side,

buy postcards, consign every stop to memory.
I'd see everything through your eyes, for the first time.

Instead I watch my gums bleed, watch the dark line
form from navel down, a

blackening arrow to crotch. Each new silver
stretch mark distracts me utterly,

I forget how soon you will arrive.
Already you have lost gills and tail,

your spine has grown its perfect column. Already I boast
of your limb buds, eyelids, ear canals,

how you are now distinguishable from kitten, tadpole,
elephant. You made your first appearance

in my body, no different from the blackberry:
same dark and glistening cluster of cells, blood-rich,

friable – I walked to get the mail, I took my pink lady-pills
and planted my feet heavily in each day's repetitions,

while you rushed to end the journey, reabsorbing
the nubs that would have become wings, briefly

taking the form of each animal you would *not* be,
free of baggage, shifting toward the shape you will finally keep

when that engine laboriously slows, puffing with steam,
when the heavy doors are thrown open to the light

and all the relatives wait with bouquets
at the end of the platform.

Wandering Womb

Painfully I have learned, achingly
    come to believe, as the ancients did,
        that the womb is unattached: wandering each night
            – hysterical little organ –
      the length of a woman's body,
capturing stray homunculi in its folds.

The first time my womb met open air,
    I was numb from the neck down;
        to check, they ran pins over my shoulders.
    My arms spread and strapped down.

        Though my lips were parched
        no one would bring me water.

Doctors sheeted the space between my face
    and that dangerous organ.
        They said the sterile barrier must
    be maintained. Watching the cut
      might make me believe
        I felt it.

        To know they could rend me in two
        and I would feel nothing: the first miracle.

Just picture the quick slit!
    Bowel shifted
        out of the way, gaudy pink garlands looped
    lustrous as a holiday display. Then

the centrepiece: baby
      tightly folded, coated in white vernix.
        The rub to flush,

fast transfer to some
more reliable oven.

      Prayer for crying,
answered.

Wet and shining as a Christmas ham,
   the womb, lifted out to have its new mouth stitched,
secrets sewed away.
      Dark placenta, what the ancients called
      cake –
sloshed in the trash
behind the blue drape.

All the weeks after, when laughter brought me to tears,
      bent me double, when the womb showed me its place
        in the primacy of my anatomy. I began to understand
what the Victorians taught

was perhaps true: If I thought too hard
      in this hysterical state about how it all began,
        infinity and conception, stretch marks
and impending death, I'd suffer Sprained Brains.

Step by aching step I came to revere the ancients:
how did they know
that at night my womb went out
to gather flowers?

Every morning I woke,
throbbing
like the princess who had stolen away
to dance holes through her slippers.

Remembering nothing of my dreams,
every morning
beginning again: breasts rolling
their vacant, milky eyes,
new scar smiling its crooked grin,
the disparate pieces of my body
bound with black thread, crusted with blood.

Beside my arm, the slumbering dark head.
To know God is
to wander,
cleft in two. To know precisely
the cost –
God
– of the wet head that fits perfectly in your hand.

Last Passover in Montreal

I.

He wakes from his nap chortling to suck, dark
hair tendrilled with dream sweat, and you thirst

the thirst of a lactating woman in April,
you are parched with fear of death, his, that last

small parcelled-out breath, the moment you
reach him, that ache in the soles of your feet rising

to envelop you. And so you sleep
with him wedged between you and the wall in the now-

sterile marital bed, damp with a fine mist of milk,
sweet Pampers, chapped skin. You sleep on edge,

on the edges of your small, gassy creation,
your milk marking a trail of drops

from the kitchen to the bedroom: Gretel's crumbs,
the salt that follows you home

after a sea voyage,
leading back to his raven chuffs,

his peacock screams. You offer yourself,
blue milk, gold cream,

you feed him, and your breasts,
dark apples, gleam.

II.

Now that you are leaving, you allow yourself
some tenderness for Montreal, now that you know

you will never spend another winter snowbound
with a colicky infant, resigned

to speaking French like the immigrant
you are. Now you walk the city gently,

he hangs from your shoulders, a bag of heat,
a lead apron, and his feet beat time

against your thighs. Lambs, hooked
in the windows of the Portuguese groceries,

pock newspapers with their blood,
Hasidic girls flit past you

in their flowered petticoats, bright butterflies
on *trottinettes*, swerving between the black-

clad Greek women with thick ankles
who block your path, brush off the dappled laugh

of the bare-chested, sweet-
nippled *pur laine* boys on rollerblades

who no longer bother trying to run you down
to make you look at them.

III.

At first your nipples sprayed blood, it foamed
out the sides of his mouth as you cracked the joints

of your feet in pain, drowning alone
on your side of the bed. He swallowed you wholly,

mouth wide as a trout, sharp bone definitive
under his gums, one leg flung over your shoulder,

casual as a tail. Slowly your anemic body
restitches its new shift. Every hour

you make your uncomprehending pilgrimage:
thirty steps from bed to crib to fridge.

What you need, you believe,
is a new city.

IV.

It's the stink of Avenue du Parc you'll miss,
stands of Caribbean mangoes, Latin avocados,

bagels sweating in brick ovens. Clean sheets
jig on the fire escapes, Hasid

schoolboys chant their lessons
through the open windows. But you are not

kosher, you are blood and milk
transfused into the one who should

outlive you. His bones knit into place,
teeth jell to opaque permanence.

You have joined the middle generation.
Your sympathies have shifted with your blood

offerings, imagining deeply for the first time
your parents as they became parents

in a city you've never visited,
your parents before the exile,

a coarse salt tossed over the shoulder.
It's hot twilight

and the baby's sleeping,
the cup of wine is far too sweet

and evening brings its own
transformations:

entitlement to gratitude,
anger to startled prayer.

The Night I Weaned You

The night I weaned you
I checked into Bienvenue B&B
and left you in arms far stronger than mine.

I ate alone, pausing between each bite, trying to recall
who I had been before you came.
I did not want company, I did not want

to go out. The TV was set to hearing-impaired
translation, and I could not switch it off.
All evening I stayed inside, watching

what I never get to see: reality TV.
The Maury show
asking me: *Is your teenage daughter*

about to get married and you think her fiancé's
cheating? Then call. Are you ready
to find out once and for all

who is the real father
of your child? Call.
Underneath, the closed-captioning ran wild,

CNN discussed wars in distant
places, and I read the mysterious translation:
fighting among Ivory Coast rib bells,

and thought how far
the world seemed from me!
All night I lay on my back, breasts pulsing

their separate migraines, blind and aching.
Very late I watched a documentary on Susan Smith
and was reassured about my own slipping

maternal instincts: the fierce, sucking love I carry
for you. In the darkness I thought of
Alex and Michael Smith,

the six minutes it took their car to sink.
All night my breasts sobbed thin tears
and I wiped and wiped their tiny, streaming mouths

with a corner of white Kleenex.
The TV flashed its lights across my skin, body
my own again, if just for a night,

while you at home, screaming for milk and solace,
learned, finally, the comfort of your thumb,
flesh of my flesh

the jingle bells of your sleepy bunny,
that you could be nourished without me,
rib of my rib

that your world extended beyond my grasp,
that another's arms could console you.

Notes on Arrival and Departure

I could live or not live; it does not matter
to be one stone more, the dark stone,
the pure stone which the river bears away.
  – Pablo Neruda, "Oh Earth, Wait for Me"

Because I am a careful woman,
or full of fear, at any rate unwilling to bet
on the constancy of any heart, I will put it
in print. Because
now it's my turn to ask the hard questions, not
why are pumpkins orange? or *why stars?*
but why do I fear death? yours most
but also my own, what would keep me
from you.

When I was wheeled into the delivery room
I told myself no matter what, this cramp
was finite; it had a beginning,
it would have an end. That
comforted me. I am not old or wise enough
to be anyone's mother, I still can't grasp
that there was a beginning before *my* beginning,
that the tale will continue without me.
Still, I am braver than I believed: knowing nothing
I decided to conceive,
and conceived.

As usual, too much is left undone.
In Vancouver, as usual, it rains,
and the pots left soaking in the sink
have reproachfully begun to stink. Then
there are all your little bottles to be reamed with soap
and set to dry on clean towels,
there are all my transparent ambitions for us both.
Nothing has changed since they handed me you,
mesh-capped, greasy and fish-eyed in a swaddle,
nothing has changed in the world since you entered it.

Who said, *None of us are free until we're all free?*
It's not like that at all, though
I guess I'll probably do okay,
live to age, and so will you
already almost two and rushing into a future
of papier mâché, summer vacations,
the usual teen resentments and then some,
with me as your mother,
arranging our dental appointments, play dates,
separating the whites from the darks,
writing in the spaces in between.

We'll go on, I mean, with our lives,
pass round our merry UNICEF cards.
While other children detonate bombs
on the hard-packed paths
leading from their homes,
we'll learn to make do
with our good luck.

And when I say nothing changed
I mean, of course, that you changed me utterly,
and though I hoped to avoid the usual things
that fond mothers say, you must know
a few truths: you may search in vain for God,
but don't doubt the love
of your big-assed, big-mouthed
personal creator, the one who gained and lost a third
of her weight for you.

Don't forget
there are ways of living worse
than simply dying, for though I fear death,
I am working on it, getting over it, I mean,
since I must show you how to do this, too,
since the best I can hope for is that you will watch me leave
as I watched you arrive, numb to pain,
with a little fear and great wonder.

When I reclined on the stretcher
the ghosts of mothers whispered
in my drugged ears, all the women
who had never risen from childbed.
The bright new instruments, sterile technique,
bold birth plan – nothing hushed them,
they crowded around the bed,
gripping me with an embrace cool and deadening as epidural,
and I was afraid, *yes*, that I would die,
though in the moment death seemed astonishing most of all.

Just at that point I found peace
though later that night I lost it. Just then,
breathing out, I gave in.
Though vaguely disappointed we hadn't met,
I was not really thinking of you.
You were still inside me, not yet yourself
and I had not yet learned
the first lesson of motherhood:
pretend you are brave
until you are brave.

SHEETS

It has all gone according to plan,
mine, made when I was ten. My mother divorced the man
who came to take the place of my father.

Every time we drove off in her cold car
I held my breath, hoping we'd go so far
we couldn't go home: *Please Mum, I can make you happy*,

but by the time she left I'd long since moved out west
and learned to love him more, or her less.
Now she comes to visit me alone, stays for a week,

hides pots in unexpected places, cooks with too much fat.
He comes for a single night, hangs up his coat and hat
and lifts his step-grandson. His face has softened with defeat,

as has her own. Each in turn asks me for news of the other,
and I tell them the parts that hurt – devious daughter –
the parts that prove they were right to part,

but finally my intentions are pure. I do not tell them how
between her visit and his I went down
with my son on one arm, clean sheets on the other, intending

to change the bed, but the smell of roses from the lotion my mother wears
drifted like a rainstorm up the stairs
and I turned,

leaving the bed as it was, awaiting his arrival:
her scent of roses a reproachful perfume, a rival
for his dream-time, a thorn –

or perhaps the scent became the dream itself: bouquet
of ivory wedding roses dried upon a shelf.

September Letters

Dear Marjan,

Blind lion, face-scarred, rib-thin,
pacing the bars of your rusty cage. And Donatella,
dear old bear, snout-wound suppurating
from the sword-slash of a Taliban,

did you not hear?
The North American experts have been called in.
Hollywood mobilizes its tax-deductible donations.
Once again our better inclinations

have been misguided, abused. Other keepers
are flown in, deals made with other zoos.
Whose fault that two animals are front-page news,
while the orphans are so numerous they remain anonymous?

Dear Mammals, what was unbearable
has become the way things are.
The Buddha is blasted to gravel,
and we must make sense of an airplane becoming flame

against the sharp hip of a building.
Some try simply to recall the name of a bear
– *O Donatella!* who once raised her broad palms in the air
and solemnly danced

for the children of Kabul,
girls clapping boldly next to their brothers,
the sun sharing its warm gifts
with them all.

Dear Mother,

I am writing without feeling, having flown from France
September 11th, your grandson bouncing
in his CAA-approved car seat, safe as milk.
I'm sorry you worried we had been exploded

those long hours you spent on hold,
consulting with the airlines,
having no idea where our plane was.
We knew nothing until we began to descend

and the pilot shared what he had kept for hours,
where we were, where we would *not* be going.
I thought, insanely, of buying a car,
of never flying again.

The airport was a mob of stranded tourists,
hushed sobs. We were stuck till 3:00 a.m.,
your grandson mercifully conked out on the luggage.
My lover comes from another country –

we would have to fly again, and soon. Just after 3:00, we got a room.

Dear Meena,

You began the women's revolution;
you were its first martyr.
I can neither forget you nor tell your story.
I'll talk instead of myself,

the modern, post-postmodern method, one soul
that cannot ever know another,
or imagine another's dreams.
Where I live, one in four Canadians

identifies as a poet. Where I live,
nobody reads poetry. Thank you for the poem
in which you wrote: *I'm the woman*
who has awoken.

You wrote: *I've said farewell to all golden bracelets.*
And then you were shot.
What did I care
until I came that close to terror?

I have dreamed a country of women
living in rooms with blackened windows.
I have imagined the blue cotton weave
through which

you viewed the world.
Pictured the soul grown thin, thin,
sunlight filtered through mesh.
Pictured the bones' hollow piping,

growing more porous each year,
more troubled. Framed your sisters
in their brightest moments, your sisters at home
blooming in darkness. Remember?

The way you flourished, nipples sweet as olives,
buried alive when the gardener grew jealous.
The way you fought: a burqa to conceal a camera,
a poem to reveal a woman's war.

Meena, forgive me for not writing before.

Dear Isabelle,

The pilot clears his throat, the overhead
clicks dead. The child between us sleeps on.
Fingertips touching, we lean back on our descent
with nothing to say. We barely bounce

on the runway. I lean into you, spiralling back
in time, back to last week, climbing Mont Saint-Michel
with our son swinging between us. Beneath
the thin blue American Airlines blanket,

when few words are necessary,
we hold on. Isabelle, thank you
for these eight years, so good
so far, for giving your seat to the stewardess in tears.

Thank you for the urgency of your love,
knowing we are not safe, though still safe enough,
in a world where our love is answered with stones.
We are decadence incarnate,

two women in comfortable shoes, we kiss cheeks
like sisters when we must, speak each other's endings,
live in relative comfort. Isabelle,
the weight of the heart under siege takes its toll.

Thank you for not letting go.

Dear Anonymous Woman Executed for Adultery in the United Nations–
Funded Sports Stadium,

Dear – What was your name? Exactly when
were you caught? Did you know where
you were being taken, does your family
know your grave plot?

Did your lover cry out, did he rend his clothes in secret?
I know the crowd watched carefully as you tripped
on the hem of your robes in the hot air
before you were shot, and fell,

in the middle of the arena to a noise, not applause,
like cicadas thrumming. I saw the film, the kohl-dark ingots,
your brain's last clotted thoughts
spilled onto your hair and shrouded head.

I saw your burqa in the dry air trembling with blood.
But I never saw your lover. Please, let it have been love,
not something violent, grown malignant
within you. Did he get away with murder?

Dear Anonymous Woman Who Filmed the Execution,

And Dear – On what food did you grow
impossibly brave? You stood
in the crowd at the stadium. God has many names
and none of them mattered.

You dared: God was your camera.
God hid under the dark-woven folds
of your required robe. God's eye
was made to record

with a small noise, hanging in the film
between your breasts, a woman's
execution curled in the undeveloped roll,
as though death had not yet

occurred. As if, were the film never processed,
you could switch past to future, correct
the present imperfect. She would not have been shot.
You would be at home, peeling an orange.

Dear Executioner,

What were you thinking as you stood
behind her, as she knelt
and you carried out the sentence,
gun in hand, followed through

on God's command? Did you
think of your wife or simply of the task?
The wind rose, briefly fingered your hair.
God is the sentence and the execution, but – Dear,

God is the lovers' brave infidelity, too, singing
long after the heat dissipates. Once
He created a garden: partridges,
almonds and pomegranates.

Oasis of song, cloistered sapling.

      Said: *Do you not know me in my nakedness?*

Said: I am the bloodstain
left in the dust after her shrouded body
is hauled away in your truck, both hands broken
behind her back.

   Said: Only the speechless hear me.
      Only the silent do not turn away.

      Do you not know me by my song?

I am the song of spilled blood, fragrant as lanolin,
as vernix from the skin of newborns,
ripe as a lemon tree
springing from the ribs of the earth.

I am the slow circle
of the bear's dance. I am the wild lions of the desert
and I am their carrion feast, too,
Marjan's blind and crusted eye. *Pray* –

For I am the pigeons that fill the twilit stadium
lifting and settling, quietly calling one another home,
drawn to that dark patch, that mineral stain
after the crowd has gone.

FREEWAY ENTRANCE, PORT MOODY

for Shelley, who found it

One day, daydreaming as her husband entered
the freeway on-ramp, she put her book down, glanced back
over her shoulder. In that fenced-in no man's land she noticed
a scattering of blue cornflowers, California poppies;
she promised herself she would return. Next week,
the Bouvier leaping joyfully ahead, she found the gap
in the fence, cabbages and runner beans flourishing
among the Scotch broom. There in the thickest part
of the blackberries: a blue tarp, thin smokestack
with vanishing smoke, empty bottles, the vinegar stink
of a bear's lair. The dog barked until she called her back,
left that wild man alone upon his chosen patch
of ground, though she stops sometimes to wonder
in what small town his parents wait for news of him,
reheating the coffee, rehashing each real or imagined mistake –

Stars

Soon
soon we shall know
if we have learned to accept that the stars
do not go out when we die.
  – Abba Kovner, "Detached Verses"

They snaked a long tube from your neck
through your arteries, opening each of the chambers

of your heart, plaqued up by years
of eating the fat I left on my plate, though you stayed strong

and fit. Remember the horse you shot that winter,
how I hated eating it? Gelding stew, gelatinous old chew,

and these tubes through your heart describe
a generational failure, as though if only I had spoken of love

more freely, eaten what you told me, if
I had finished all the stories you stopped writing –

understood the unspoken endings – you'd be well.
Your body the colour of crushed iris

from the slow weeping of blood beneath your skin.
I have forgotten nothing. Not the time you broke your back

falling from the scaffolds of your boat
and your men rowed you across the channel in the dark.

There is nothing you've feared that you haven't tried:
fear is your ultimatum. Of course

your heart was clogged, all your courage
appeared to me as rage, and I could not trust you.

As a child I lacked imagination or context to see you,
Father, as a child once, holding hands with your twin

who vowed to be a shepherdess while you, you dreamed
of shuttles combing the stars, you dreamed of walking on the moon,

a tube in your mouth to breathe the precious air tanked on your back,
your blood rich with oxygen, and though you are earthbound still,

the mask is right, the whiteness of the sheets
is otherworldly, and your thinned blood

rockets through your stent as we gaze out the window
at the slow progress of stars casting their lights,

stars born a hundred million years before,
and already dead

when their light reaches us, the achingly slow
progress of illumination.

Raccoons in Garbage

Some nights, I've nearly
caught them.

This afternoon, interrupted
by a ceramic pot knocked off the deck,
I put aside my books
and saw them, a team of three
beneath the porch, attacking the green-black sacks
with their neat hands.

Out came the small stained napkins
used to catch my monthly blood
and the blood of packaged meat.
Out came the grapefruit rinds, disposable diapers,
coffee grounds, nylons with runs,
eggshells in a small stack,
hollow monument to Wednesday's
omelette.

The stooges snickered
behind their bandit masks as they sorted
the offal from the meal. I forgot to be annoyed,
so curious I finally abandoned my body,
all but the observant eye
I seek but never find in meditation.

As soon as I recognized its scent,
whatever it was,

being or *not-being*,
lifted its sharp nose,
sensed a trap, slipped under the fence
and was gone: one dark shape
shadowing the others.

Alone with the remnants,
the sheerest glimpse of grace,
throbbing, wild as any beast,
I knelt to sweep away the feast.

ENVOY TO A POEM NEVER SENT

Was it you who came   kimi ya koshi
or was it I who went?   ware ya yukikemu
I do not remember . . .   omoezu
    – a woman writing to her lover after their night together,
    Tales of Ise (Ise monogatari)

In Japanese one cormorant-black night, I learned from my lover
that the phrase for coming was going.

I'm going, won't you please accompany me this evening as I wander?
I'm going. I don't know if I'll be back. Would you like a lock

of my barbarian yellow hair, keepsake to our taboo affair
in these silent shouji-screened rooms? No one thinks to look

for you here, married woman and mother of two, your daughter
near my age, your hair streaked with grey. What can we learn from

this night of cicadas and linguistics? What am I to make
of the stretch marks gleaming on your belly, the mercury of your lips

slipping under my thumbs, unstoppable, beading
unstable element, rising with the heat? What am I to reply

when you tell me you are going? Let me hold the silver in your hair.
I'm coming. I also must go.

THE EXECUTION OF FORM: A HISTORY LESSON

The young man who took the horses out for pasture found near the lake an Indian girl about eight years old. The little girl was perfectly naked, her long black hair was matted, and she was covered with scars from head to feet. She could only make a pitiful moaning noise. Dr. Truman Bonney, my uncle, examined her and said she was suffering from hunger and that the flies had almost eaten her up. Near by we could see where two tribes of Indians had fought. She had apparently crept to one side, out of danger, and had been left. . . . A council among the men was held to see what should be done with her. My father wanted to take her along; others wanted to kill her and put her out of her misery. . . . A vote was taken and it was decided to do nothing about it, but to leave her where we found her. My mother and my aunt were unwilling to leave the little girl. They stayed behind to do all they could do for her. When they finally joined us their eyes were red and swollen from crying. . . . Mother said she had knelt down by the little girl and had asked God to take care of her. One of the young men in charge of the horses felt so badly about leaving her, he went back and put a bullet through her head and put her out of her misery.

– Recalled by Benjamin Franklin Bonney, who was seven years old in 1844, the year he travelled to California with his family

1. Near the Lake

*"The young man who took the horses out for pasture found near the lake an
Indian girl about eight years old."*

A clump of cattails to piss on,
the horses' leather leads dangling in the water.

A blue heron, awkward on her backward
knees, plucking escargots from the reeds.
Slate wingspan as he staked out the horses,
trail of lake water dripping
from her slim-boned feet to the far shore.

His leather boots sucked water
as he stepped from one mat of weeds
to another. Thin horses cropped the sharp
marsh grass, pack sores on their withers crusting
in the sun, bloody and raw as California territory.
Withers in constant irritated twitch
as the horseflies landed and bit.
Back home they would have been shot for mercy.

Signs of battle: black water titrated
with blood. Clump of dark hair on the grass, too fine
and shining to have come from any horse.
A small hatchet. Broken blade.

And, of course he found you,
standing naked among the rushes.
Young man holding ruined horses,

pride-cleaned guns. You were his first
naked girl. You were his first
Indian. You were the first time he'd seen
his mother cry since they buried her stillborn.

You stood like Narcissus near the dark water
where you were abandoned. Nobody's daughter.

2. Songs in the Blankets of Pilgrims

"The little girl was perfectly naked, her long black hair was matted, and she was covered with scars from head to feet."

Sparks from your mother's fire marked
your thighs. Scarlet fever scarred in stars.
Dogbite's white-toothed memory wrapped your ankle.
Blackberry brambles sliced your shoulders
and dried.

And the new wounds that suppurate,
draw flies? Incomprehensible as the new
songs rising from pioneer campfires,
the ones you watched, unseen, abandoned. Songs
that flickered from one wagon bed to the next,
and sounded utterly unlike what you called music,
music from Ghana and Cork to Georgia, to Salem,
carried like smallpox rolled in the blankets of pilgrims,
shaken and spread across California, to your listening ears:

> *Dark girl, dark girl, don't lie to me,*
> *Tell me where did you sleep last night?*
> *In the pines, in the pines, where the sun never shines*
> *And I shivered the whole night through.*

The truth? The truth in a net of scars.

3. What Time Will Say

"She could only make a pitiful moaning noise."

They heard you moan before they turned away.
Their compromise was simply to turn and go.
What is it you were trying to say?

Two women stayed behind and knelt to pray
as water seeped through dirty calico.
They heard you moan before they walked away.

Perhaps your ghost is seriously inclined to stay.
Your voice in the rushes still calls to your mother, although
what you were trying to say

was never understood. Pray for us. Pray.
Hang your head over, hear the wind blow
They heard you moan before they turned away.

Your cuts were wet with blood, hair pocked with clay.
And likely you would not have lived even so.
What is it you were trying to say?

Perhaps your mother died coming home that day.
Perhaps your soul is at peace; I would not know.
And still you moaned and still they turned away.
What is it you were trying to say?

4. Flysong

"Dr. Truman Bonney, my uncle, examined her and said she was suffering from hunger and that the flies had almost eaten her up."

Houseflies, horseflies, bluebottles,
mosquitoes, deerflies, whiteflies, gnats. All convene,
preferring the dark pools of your eyes
to any still water. Buzz for your salt, whine
across your twilit skin, eat the yellow crusts of sleep
from your inner canthus. They come, each of them
for their ounce of flesh, they rut, they sow and reap
upon the torment of your cuts.
You have given up brushing them away.
You have been standing in this place
for two nights and three days. You have tried to pray.
You are waiting for your mother to come and clean your face

with her saliva, with her rough fingers. *Shoo, fly, don't bother me.*
I belong to somebody.

5. Ballad of the Indian Girl

"She had apparently crept to one side, out of danger, and had been left."

We left you behind in the wet grass
but you still seek my dreams.
You are the scent of the sage I pass
between my fingers, pungent and clean.

You were my age then. Now I'm old.
I'm too late. The rosemary, blue-eyed
under resinous weight, falls to one side.
Morning glories hide

their white throats. The bones
of the dead rot clean. Wet soil
clots my spade as I strike rock, turn. Alone
with a garden gone wild, this toil

burns, reliable as your ghost, pungent as sage.
Your body became a temple of flies
while I lived to age. When I cried that day
Papa said, *Ben, she was bound to die.*

Mama said, *Pray.* Uncle said,
*In San Francisco you'll eat horehound candy
and white bread every day.*

6. In the Rye

"My father wanted to take her along; others wanted to kill her and put her out of her misery."

Jack and Gye
Went out in the Rye
And they found a little girl with one black eye.
Come, says Jack, let's knock her on the head.
No, says Gye, let's buy her some bread.
You buy one loaf and I'll buy two
and we'll bring her up as other folk do.

7. Prayer

*"When they finally joined us their eyes were red and swollen from crying.
... Mother said she had knelt down by the little girl and had asked God to
take care of her."*

Our Lady of the Covered Wagons
Our Lady of the Oxen
Our Lady of the Campfire
Our Lady of Laudanum
Our Lady of Tick Fever
Our Lady of Migraine & Trepanation
Our Lady of Gold Dust,
Dropped Uterus,
Our Lady of Tumbleweed,
mother who lost a child. *Selah.*
We walk in the brackish waters, we wash
without a flake of soap, we mark our graves
with piled rock, leave a stillborn in the earth
and ride away, still bleeding afterbirth.

Lord: We have followed the Patriarchs
into the desert. The hominy cakes have been baked
with obedience. The marriage quilts have been sewn.
We have lain down. We have been delivered.

We entrust her to Your care. *Selah.*
The wagons are leaving. We would keep her
if we dared. Your condors are closing in.
Your swamp has disgusted our hems.

8. The Horse Boy

"One of the young men in charge of the horses felt so badly about leaving her, he went back and put a bullet through her head and put her out of her misery."

Stood too close as he shot. Some of your brains splattered his boots. He wiped them on the wet grass. Later, when they had to cross the desert and they ran out of water, he remembered this wet place, you toppling into the wild iris. All around him were bawling oxen falling to their knees and unable to rise. He went among them offering bullets. The rifle blasted its dark-barrelled gifts until the only noise was children moaning in their wagon beds. His mother gave each of the little ones a flattened bullet to suck, to engage their mouths with the memory of coolness. For four days they wandered in the desert and he thought of the Israelites, the promised land. He sometimes wished he'd kept you. It was lonely crossing the desert, driving the two horses that hadn't died. After the sun fell, his bones chilled. He leaned against the pinto pony as he walked, warmed his hands against her black and pink teats. She gave him her warm breath. The horse boy was certain that his suffering was being noted. He believed, as each of us does, that he was marked for greatness, that he was destined for love.

Because your new wife
is expecting and there isn't enough,

take your girl and boy into the woods
but do it regretfully, with love,

three times, because they keep coming home,
their hands full of gingerbread and bones.

Birth one a year for seven years, each brain
shrunk like a walnut in its shell

because of your love for alcohol. Condemn them
to that life, then give them away.

Because it's not clearly a boy, castrate it,
carve it a second os, going nowhere,

buy it pink slippers and a new name.
Put him in a bulrush basket and set him

in the river, hoping Pharaoh's daughter will wish
to bathe that day. Snuff out the infant

as soon as she arrives,
because she's a girl and you don't need a girl.

Heave him to a pyre, because God
is whimpering in your ear.

Slaughter a ram on his chest instead,
blood manacling your hands.

Because, God help you, you were fifteen
and the Song of Songs was in you

again. You stood behind his car
after, looking at the stars as he lifted your hair,

gently pushed your earring
back through the lobe.

Because you created them, they are yours
to destroy. You only wanted,

you simply had to make him stop screaming.
Because you were sure your daughter

would forgive you for the Beast.
Because someone you loved gave you

a red hood. Because the piper
stepped out of the woods,

promised you a song for playing his pipe.
Because a little man pulled up your dress,

and it was *not*, he said,
to spank you, though you were very naughty,

it was the better to love you, my dear.
Because you cried wolf and no one believed you.

Because you stepped off the path
and felt smaller than a bluebell.

Because it was done to you once,
a long time ago,

in rooms of stone so thick
there was no echo. You were in the woods,

picking wild strawberries, and someone
called you by name.

Because their bodies are unblemished
and your hands are alive with pain.

ALGERIAN WOMAN MOURNING (1997 PHOTO OF THE YEAR)

Light has made white lilies of her cheeks,
her neck a fistful of stems
bursting with chords of grief
he felt compelled to capture.
Someone older – her mother? – presses
breastbone and shoulders between rough hands,
to contain her. To keep her here.

Because one could ascend on such wings of pain.

Outside the Zmirli hospital in Algiers
the morning after the massacre,
the French photographer
leans against the shadowed wall,
his shutter snaps light over her face.
For this he will win an award, some money
which must be delivered anonymously
because he fears for his life.
For her: nothing.

Back in his country, safe,
he has had hours to study her face
in his darkroom. The small grey bulb of her sternum,
half moons of her eyes, a mouth full of darkness,
gasp of white teeth, blue veil slipping off her hair.

Still she stands, alive in the harsh morning.
The night torn apart by men who spread terror,

who carved the deaths of her eight children
into the lines of her face, spilled their screams
into the packed earth outside her door.

No more arrhythmia
of a child's handclaps on a stone wall, no cereal
boiling over the side of the iron pot.

Prayer of ten thousand diapers wrung and washed.

Her mouth, bitter from dehydration,
opens to a gasp of orange blossom, fetid
almond, and the flash stutters its white doves
across her body. To be spared is not
to know mercy.

To Those I Entrusted With Memorizing My Poems

I am Anna, mother to a single son
who grows middle-aged in a Leningrad prison.
I watched each poet I love condemned,
watched the books of poems burn.

I'm Akhmatova. When I was young, men
swarmed thick as flies, drawn to my pale eyes, dark hair,
my height, exotic lineage to Genghis Khan.
The way I came to them at night, sweet nightmare

bringing in the cold, a few wet
flakes of snow on my furs. But that is not why
I have called you here. Being unable to forget
or ignore my awful muse, I write, I

continue to write. Because of my caged son,
I'm forced to lock each verse in my mind.
I have turned from the frozen page, chosen
you to remember my words. You will, from time to time

be summoned; I will test your memory.
Should you ask why you were thus encumbered,
I will answer simply: Because you are here. Because you know me.
Because I find you honest in a country torn asunder

by betrayals. Do not think, as I have thought,
waiting in line with others outside the prison
these nights where I shift from foot to frozen foot,
that we are chosen for no good reason.

Requiem: Quatsino Burning

Sebastian Daniel Larson Handel, 1990–2002
Roxanne Alexandra Jex Handel, 1992–2002
Martial Maxfield Brindley-Rose Handel, 1994–2002
Moriah Selene Vesta-Rose Siegler Handel, 1996–2002
Levi Liam Felix Zaccheus Woods Handel, 1997–2002
Lydia Sophia Gale Zipphora Woods Handel, 1999–2002

Ash fine as wheaten hair climbs the pines and alders,
smoulders in the air. The first day she struck back at their father
was when he told all six were dead, his revenge for her leaving.

Dead. Strangled by his hands, then burned along with her house.
Still her breasts foolishly shed their blind milk
for her youngest as she sits in her hospital bed, both hands

bandaged on the crumpled spread. She rests with nothing to do
for the first time in a decade, she eats the sedatives,
folds the paper cup. Loss congeals in her breasts,

veined and tight as green apples. Her house cooked down
like a sauce, six children in its smokebound
heart, hard glaze to ash. She wonders what she will do

when the resin on her nipples dries and falls away, who she'll be
when the curtain around her bed is ripped free
and she must walk out of the fluorescence and see.

The Graduate Record Exam is full of irrelevant questions, making it particularly tedious to take. If, however, it were rewritten with an emphasis on what matters, how many more of us would pursue higher and yet higher education?

1. Write an essay on why the most popular TV channel during Christmas is the picture of the Yule log burning.

2. North American adults replace their dining-room table on average as often as they replace their spouse – 1.5 times in a lifetime. Discuss.

3. The question elementary-school children most want to ask about sexual intercourse is just how long the penis needs to stay in the vagina to make a baby. The reason behind this is frightening conversations they've overheard: *Aunt Helen and Uncle Dave have been trying for* five years *to have a baby.* Explain how time changes over time.

4. Sally and Liz were lovers for seven years. Sally's new lover, Kiera, is throwing a potluck. Liz is coming with Anne, the woman she left Sally for. Anne's ex, Samara, will also be coming. Samara is having a secret affair with Kiera. Samara's lover, Beth, remains bitter over her breakup with Anne; she will attend with Ashley. How must Kiera seat everyone so that none of the women leave the potluck in tears?

5. Twenty-four million people in Africa are infected with HIV. Mothers who breast-feed have a thirty per cent chance of infecting their infants. Mothers who don't breast-feed have less than a six per cent chance.

However, the greatest risk to small children in Africa is dysentery due to unsanitary drinking water. Therapy to reduce HIV transmission between mother and nursing child could be made available for the cost per capita of a Starbucks Venti Caramel Latte. What percentage of Americans would consider donating this cost? What percentage would abstain from caramel at least?

6. Why do the crazy become obsessed with God? Discuss, giving examples from Russian Literature.

7. The average worker bee gathers a thimbleful of honey in her lifetime. The most precious Persian carpets were a life's work for the girls imprisoned their entire lives to hook a single carpet.

a) Express the value of the carpet in an inverse ratio to the value of the girls.

b) Calculate the weight of each girl to the nearest thimbleful of honey.

8. When the atom bomb Einstein helped to create was dropped on Hiroshima, he covered his eyes with his hands and said, "Vey ist Mir" (Woe is Me). In an earlier letter to his wife, he had written, "You are neither to expect intimacy nor to reproach me in any way," though he ended up leaving her even so. Einstein was chosen by *Time* as "Man of the Century."

a) Create a differential equation for lives lost in Hiroshima divided by memorial lanterns cast in the Motoyasu River, factoring in the phrase "Never Again," to explain Rwanda.

b) If a child asked you, "Well, then, what good is it to be smart?" how would you answer this question?

69

MORNING PAPER

This is the photograph: blonde boy, one shoulder back,
hurling a brick through a window.
It was after a game, hockey, I think.
All the other looters ran
from the cameraman, but this blue-eyed boy,
jeans slung low on his hips,
was not so shy.

Looting, says my father,
burying his face in his hands.
But looting art supplies, says my stepmother,
working her small shard of hope
under his skin. *But looting*, he groans again, meaning

Not my boy: yours. *He didn't even
have the sense to run*, he tells me. I pour orange juice,
the good child. Only one of us can do this.
My stepmother percolates a second pot.
Sunshine fingers dust motes in
my father's hair.

This is the *Daily Sun* and he
is front-page news. We are the family behind
the scenes, the context
unconsidered. All over the city
people work the rubber bands off their papers,
drop their glances on his unseeing face.

We are the shock on the face of the art shop's owner
at 8:00 a.m. Broken glass, splintered brushes,
the bright violet and scarlet of burst oils
freezing in the mud.

The phone bawls, spills my father's second cup.
Even locked up, the boy's still raging, not yet feeling
his broken hand. My stepmother turns her front-page son
face down, puts on a sweater
to fend off morning's chill.
My father gets his keys to go post bail.

LOVE'S FIRST DECADE

For Isabelle

Though we were young when we met,
we've grown younger recently.
Perhaps it's the fault of the child – we're not playing
house any more. We've grown
more certain of each other, though less
of everything else, in these, what you call
our "compromised thirties." We no longer believe
that we have an endless number
of lives to try on, that we can change as often
as we wish, as though rehearsing for prom night,
unhooking one pastel gown
for another. This singular path
is the one we have taken: this love,
this child, and no other.

See how we have grown into this efficient
family machine, interdependent
ecosystem, breathing in
one another's air, sharing the labour.

Finally we have relearned what our son
has not yet forgotten: that time is not linear, that dinosaurs
are indeed one of the great mysteries, that bones
can turn to stone and leave behind
stories. At last we have learned
it is wiser to close a door

than clean a room. Now
we are sensible enough, when we meet in the hallway
after settling him down for sleep, folding
the tiny socks, setting aside
the unmatched,

to open our arms to each other,
needing neither music nor sequins to dance.

SEQUIN

The trapeze artist who is also my girlhood friend Ruby
appears sequined in red leotards, leaping to bow
before the crowd. My breath catches, my palms grow wet
as she climbs fist over fist to seize the trapeze.

She flies faster and higher, soaring above
ordinary life, red sequined cap fracturing the light, brave
as Amelia Earhart, having turned away from men, women,
everything but the call to wing.

Hanging by an ankle, she flings herself from one swing
to another, descends, suddenly, to applause,
leaps lightly through her bows and disappears.
Backstage, rib cage still heaving with breath,

face painted with rouge and glitter, she kisses me
and two channels of blood pour from her nose.
She blows, steps back, again blows, red peonies appear
in the white tissues that fall from her chapped hands

to mingle with the roses on her chair.
For a moment I hold her hands:
terrible, blunt tools deformed to leather gloves,
talons that make flight possible. Her only love

transcendence, from this earth to the upper air.
At home I find a bead of her blood hung in my yellow hair.

74

Cirque du Soleil

You have one life.
Why not spend every day
mimicking the falcon, carving
the air? O hawk-heeled hanger,
silver-scapula'ed on your spinning
swing, hands thick as bark. Sing!

Morning and evening I pray:
transport me from my one life one-third finished,
from my two closed wounds, breathing quietly
at home under someone else's watch, blood beating
beneath their fragile occipitals.

This evening as I curled my eyelashes
before the circus, a storm blew up from
Spanish Banks. My son ran onto the porch
naked with his toy syringe: *Mama,*
I'm going to suck up the thunder
to look at under the microscope!
Applause is a stinging rain.

Help me, as I sit in the expectant dark
with the ordinary audience, to claim what
I need: darkness with a single light
shining on one man inside the German wheel
reverberating on the floor, a giant silver coin
I want to take in my mouth. Now air-hung, now
leaping between the rungs, dolphin

through his gleaming hoop, da Vinci's man
rolling across the stage in his perfect circle,
going, going, gone.

A man and a woman dressed in thin cloth
emerge from a birth of hands. They wear
the colour of skin, balance on one another, spine
to spine. He holds her taut body
above him: man as waiter,
woman as platter. Her eyes half-closed,
mouth open to the grapes of the air.

A woman with flame-blue eyelids and a mouth the colour
of pain lifts her legs over her
shoulders, skins her lips over her teeth,
takes in the whole knobbed barre
and balances, wrestling without moving,
rib cage wild as a bellows
while the audience
swallows.

You have one life, insists the woman
who hoists herself up a red silk curtain
tall as a castle. She emerges in full flight,
transformed in the free fall, bouncing
high in the still air, dangling broken
from the cord at her middle. The man beside me
lifts his shining face as the woman pulls herself
into a slip-knot, bows her head and quietly
hangs herself.

Next to my shoulder: the silence
of your weeping, grope for my hand.
Who among this vast and listening audience
has not wished for neck cords stronger than the point
where the give leaves the rope? Wished to emerge
with hope intact in the body, to prove
as she does, floating offstage on her unbroken spine –
O moth cocooned in flame – that with enough legerdemain
you can fool the hangman.

On our return, the baby,
irritated by my long absence, buckles her tongue
around my nipple, tipples, eyes rolling back
as she knocks my heart to bring down the milk,
to hear the echo she's made in me.

Later, dry heat becomes wet
as we grapple through our own silent
performances. The circus tent of the night
collapses its silk, cuts off the light,
the baby's fist lifts, spills like a lily: *O
ecstasy. O sweet-slumbering audience.
One life!* My palm stifles your mouth.

The lawyer pivots on his polished heel.
"Weigh these, I ask you: Sarah's laugh
against the flood. Sodom, city of white stone,
rubbled. That sick game of cat and mouse
he played with Abraham, just to see how far
one father, slightly unhinged, would go. The camps,
the barbed wire, and him, watching us all
to see how far we would go.

"In these chambers he has told you, *I was young.*
It was a long time ago. Ladies and gentlemen:
Arrogance! Has he ever
simply said he was sorry?"

God leans forward in his seat, blue Egyptian cotton shirt
stained with nervous sweat. "Wait," he cries.
"Understand me: I was an adolescent,
a child, really, in God years – dog years times infinity –"
He chuckles at his joke. Stone faces wait him out.
"Hear me! Like wine I have improved
with age. I gave you the leopard, the lunar eclipse,
taught you to harvest the sweet toil
of the honeybee. I have brought forgiveness
into the lemon groves of the world.
You need me. For what other desire
would you write such books,
raise such cathedrals?"

The lawyer for the people is not amused.
"He tells you *I created more
than I destroyed*. But why
should he be exempt from justice?
Because of his residence?"

The psychological expert witness stands
and takes her vow, hand on a blank
black book. "Typical," she sniffs.
"Thinks he's more important
than everyone else. Abusive. Poor
anger management.
Tries to control everything:
the grain of sand, the sparrow."

God clears his throat, indignant:
"I gave you gravity, rainstorms,
I made the many-stomached cow, taught
her to bellow, and now
you want me to be *nice*,
you want me to make all of you *behave*?"

His public defender presses his arm, whispers,
"I think we'd do better
if you'd keep your mouth shut."
He pictures her rouged mouth
ravaged by leprosy, has to sit
on his terrible hands.

The jury returns. The judge pounds his gavel.
God is sentenced to Life

as the courtroom claps, breaks into Hallelujah stomps.
The ringlets on his chiselled head tremble
as he studies his knuckles, and in the wings
his mother in her blue Easter hat
bursts into tears.

The Story

Father, tell me about the cormorant fishers,
how they dive from the boat rims
through the black sea, how they hunger
for the fish they catch but cannot swallow
past the hemp rope knotted around their necks.

Tell me again about the divers on the other side
of the Pacific, daughters of fishermen, girls who thought
nothing of not breathing for minutes on end,
who bound their black hair and never got
the salt entirely out. How they rose,
hands full of pearls, of abalone,
bodies slicked with grease,
knives glinting back their reflected grins.

Tell me of the gape and rip of the shark's jaw,
the scream of the single seal
dragged under to drown. Sing to me a little
of the sea turtle with its melancholy eyes,
of the sand-dollar currency and how you finally grew sick
of king crab, salmon's stink. Don't forget
the grey whales who swam to meet your boat,
breaking through the skin of their world
to glimpse ours, the way they called to each other,
and you, lying in your bunk, wet wool steaming,
heard their song.

Father, ask me,
and I'll tell you what it's like
to be the daughter of a fisherman
who left for Alaska every summer as the salmon ran,
slept with the gutstink of Pink and Coho between
his fingers. I'll tell you that eighty per cent
of what I love in this world can be traced
to the sea. Each element beneath the skin
retains this memory.

I'll speak of the cormorants,
how every time I pass the cliffs
they foul chalkwhite – the cliffs
where they build their nests so they can keep
their black watch on the sea –
the fine hairs rise on my skin,
thrilled, the way I shivered when you waved
the last goodbye
and the ropes were thrown from the dock.

Listen: my daughter was born with the sea
in her lungs, drowning as they towed her out.
My inheritance: the suctioning,
the tubes, the fierce thrash toward breath.
I, too, have come back
from that place. Now I walk the beach at Jericho
with her bound to my chest, small fists waving,
chuffing until the milk is pulled from deep within
and runnels down my front. The sunlight is sharp as needles
after weeks indoors in hospital.

Today I saw my second wild octopus.
It was dead, not hauled red and furious onto our small boat,
hooked by accident or miracle in your nets,
slipping off the deck and back to the sea
quick as a trick of the wet eye.

Today, it was ghostly and huge, sloshing
back and forth in time with the waves. Sun caught
its graceful pale legs unfurling
and seawater lifted them, rows of delicate flushed sake cups
beautiful in death, translucent, filled with light,

and in me something rose in reply, drinking to
that moment where all is wild – *L'Chaim!*
how we came from the sea, how we will return.

ACKNOWLEDGEMENTS

My thanks to the editors of the following publications in which these poems first appeared, many in slightly altered forms: *Grain*: "Woman Being Transfused by a Goat," "Dark Flags," and "The Proof," *Poetry*: "Sheets," *The Malahat Review*: "Stars," *Arc*: "Algerian Woman Mourning," *The New Quarterly*: "The Story," *The Spoon River Poetry Review*: "Passing Through Evolution" and "Last Passover in Montreal."

"What Time Will Say" was inspired by W.H. Auden's villanelle "If I Could Tell You."

The excerpt on page 50 is taken from *Recollections of Benjamin Franklin Bonney*, as quoted in *Pioneer Children on the Journey West* by Emmy E. Werner, published by Westview Press.

I am grateful to the Canada Council and B.C. Arts Council for the grants that sustained me while writing this collection.

My heartfelt thanks as well to my parents, Bob and Mary, Jim and Shelley, and to my uncle Herman, who got me started on this path, and who continue to inspire and support me. To Masarah, for your clear vision and willingness to go the distance, and to Sue, who always finds the right word at the right time. To the Seven Sisters writing group, who provided literary companionship and sisterhood. To Nathalie Cooke, staunch supporter and friend; and to my astonishing editor, Marlene Cookshaw, and to Ellen Seligman, thank you. I am indebted to you all.

My beloved Isabelle, and my Benjamin (who wishes I'd written a book about parrots instead), my baby, Gabrièle Inès – to you three who make every poem possible, every day a gift, my love and gratitude.